HOW TO BUILD
Birdhouses
and Feeders

HOW TO BUILD

Birdhouses

and Feeders

*Featuring 11 step-by-step
woodworking projects*

S TEPHEN M OSS *WITH*
A LAN & G ILL B RIDGEWATER

POPULAR WOODWORKING BOOKS
Cincinnati, Ohio

First published in North America
in 2001 by Popular Woodworking Books
an imprint of F&W Publications, Inc.
1507 Dana Avenue
Cincinnati, OH 45207
1-800-289-0963

ISBN 1-55870-582-1

Editorial Direction: Rosemary Wilkinson
Project Editor: Kate Latham
Production: Caroline Hansell
American Editors: Diane Schmitz and Kathi Howard

Designed and created for New Holland by AG&G Books
Design: Glyn Bridgewater
Illustrators: Alan and Gill Bridgewater
Project design: Alan Bridgewater
Photography: Ian Parsons
Editor: Fiona Corbridge
Woodwork: Alan and Gill Bridgewater, William Del Tufo

Reproduction by PICA Colour Separation, Singapore
Printed and bound by Times Offset (M) Sdn. Bhd.

The information in this book is true and complete to the best of our knowledge.
All recommendations are made without guarantee on the part of the authors and the
publishers. The authors and publishers disclaim any liability for damages or injury
resulting from the use of this information.

Dedication

*Alan and Gill would like to dedicate this book to cousin Colin and his wife Wynn
– both keen bird-watchers and wildlife gardeners.*

CONTENTS

INTRODUCTION

Sometimes when we're walking in the countryside, we stop and sit down to watch birds for a while – a robin pecking at the crumbs from our sandwiches, a thrush picking blackberries, a

kestrel hovering overhead, or perhaps even swallows swooping and diving to catch flies. It's incredibly exciting to see the sheer variety of birds, their beautiful colors, and their fascinating movements. And then when we are in the workshop carving a slab of green oak, or whittling

Scraps of food left over from your picnic sandwiches are a guaranteed way of attracting a wide variety of interesting and unusual birds.

a stick with a knife, we marvel at the pure pleasure of creating objects from wood.

So there you have it... bird-watching and woodworking – two of the most popular hobbies of all time. This book has been written to share with you the joy of working with wood, and the delight of enticing birds into your garden. It is for woodworkers who are interested in birds, and bird-watchers who want to build birdhouses in order to attract

A bird bath is not only an attractive garden feature in its own right – watching the birds bathing is a fascinating and instructive way of learning about bird behavior.

birds to the garden. It features satisfyingly creative

woodworking, which brings with it the added

Building birdhouses and feeders is a great way to spend your free time; watching the birds use them is an added pleasure.

bonus of encouraging a greater variety of birds into your garden,

giving you birdsong to listen to in the morning, and the enjoyment

of feeding birds in the winter... so much fun!

Part 1

BIRDS IN YOUR GARDEN

Birds are some of the most visible and easily observed of all living creatures – and where better to watch their habits than in your own garden? By providing food and nest sites for birds, you can enjoy their antics and behavior, as well as providing a valuable service for the birds themselves. In winter, the food we supply can mean the difference between life and death for small birds. In spring and summer, bird boxes can help many species to raise their families. We can watch and learn all year round.

ATTRACTING BIRDS TO YOUR GARDEN

A carefully considered, well-designed, wildlife-friendly garden is a series of "mini habitats", each of which provides a relatively safe place for birds to feed, shelter, roost or nest. Large, mature trees attract woodland birds, flowering plants produce seeds and are a beacon for insects, herbaceous borders provide food and ground cover, while wide areas of lawn are ideal for the more adventurous feeders.

The hawthorn provides berries from late summer until the following April, making it a very valuable food plant for thrushes and Blackbirds.

Not all gardens are large enough to include all these habitats. But even the smallest urban plot can provide enough food and shelter to create a little oasis for the birds. Wherever you live, and irrespective of the size of your garden, you can do all sorts of things to make it appeal to your local birdlife. You'll be amazed at the difference a few simple adjustments can make.

Let part of your garden "go wild"

A neatly manicured garden, where flowers are deadheaded the minute they are past their best, and shrubs are clipped back with enthusiasm, is the last thing birds want. So allow at least part of your garden to "go wild", providing a wealth of seeds and insects for birds to feed on, and a wider choice of places to nest and roost. If you're really keen on attracting birds, why not plant a wild flower meadow, using native seed varieties obtainable from reputable garden centers.

Plant "food plants"

Birds love berry-bearing plants such as elder, hawthorn, honeysuckle, cotoneaster, pyracantha and yew – and they're attractive to look at as well.

Put out food

A reliable supply of food can be the difference between survival and death for many small birds.

Provide water

Water is just as important as food, so treat the birds to a bird bath for washing and drinking.

Make a garden pond

If you have the room, another way to provide water is by making a pond. Ponds also encourage all manner of wildlife, another useful food resource for birds.

Bird heaven – not only does this garden have a bird bath, but it is sitting in a pond – it's the perfect place for birds to drink, bathe and feed.

A design for a bird-friendly garden

Hedges provide fruit and cover for nesting

Fruit trees are a good source of food

Wild area provides a variety of seeds for food

Nesting box mounted on garden shed

A pile of logs will host lots of tasty bugs

Composter provides food scraps

Large mature tree attracts woodland birds and is a good site for nestboxes

Shrubbery for nesting

Evergreen bushes and trees for winter shelter

Large lawn area

Pond attracts insects for birds

Bird bath located in an open space

Perches

With careful planning, a garden can be a haven for birds. Features such as ponds, large trees and flower borders provide much-needed cover and food.

Annuals provide seeds

Feeding table

Patio has unobstructed views of the garden

Plant shrubs and bushes for nesting
Some garden birds won't use nestboxes, but you can still help them by making sure your garden has a selection of dense shrubs where they can nest safely.

Keep out pests
Squirrels love bird food, so use squirrel-proof feeders. But the real villains are cats, which kill millions of birds. Turn to page 17 for ideas on minimizing this carnage.

Keep notes on what you see
Get a desk diary and note which birds you see, and when. Years later you can look back at your diary and draw pleasure from recalling long-forgotten sightings.

Enjoy the birds!
Gardening shouldn't be hard work all the time! Why not dig a little and then watch the birds... trim a little and then watch the birds... weed a little and then...

FEEDING GARDEN BIRDS

Providing a regular supply of different foods is one of the best ways of encouraging a variety of bird species to come into your garden. In Part 3 we look at a range of designs for bird feeders, from a simple peanut feeder to a really elaborate feeding station that will have the birds coming back for more. But before you get out the toolbox, read this section to discover which foods are suitable for stocking the feeder.

Feed regularly

There's nothing worse for the birds than discovering a garden full of food, then coming back a week later to find that the supply has run out. During the winter months especially, small birds need to feed almost every minute of the day during daylight hours, or they run the risk of starving to death. So once you start feeding them, don't stop.

Provide variety

Variety is the spice of life – for birds as well as humans. Different species have very different food requirements. Ideally you need to provide peanuts, seeds, grains, suet and other fat, fruit – such as apples – and a variety of specialized foods, such as mealworms.

Keep it clean

Stale, leftover food can soon go moldy, attracting pests and possibly causing disease, so make sure you clear away leftovers every couple of days, and give your bird table and feeders a good clean every few weeks.

Buy from a reputable source

Make sure the food you put out is suitable for wild birds by buying it from a reputable dealer (many do mail order) or from one of the bird protection groups. If the food is in any way less than perfect – stale, moldy, sour, or tainted with chemicals – then reject it.

Bird feeders are an essential addition to the garden, especially during the winter, when they provide a valuable supplement to the birds' natural diet.

GOOD FOODS FOR GARDEN BIRDS

There is now a huge and somewhat bewildering variety of different foods available, from basic peanuts and seeds (which are suitable for a wide range of birds) to specialized foods for individual species. Some of the best foods are listed below. Apart from specially bought foods, kitchen scraps will go down well with your garden birds: anything from bread to bacon, cooked rice and grated cheese. Starlings are also partial to pet food! Fresh fruit is popular with blackbirds, starlings and thrushes. If you have doubts about the suitability of foods, then do not put them out.

Peanuts: *Make sure that you put them in a suitable feeder, so that small birds cannot choke on whole nuts. Use fresh raw (unroasted and unsalted) peanuts.*

Sunflower seeds: *Like peanuts, sunflower seeds are popular with a wide variety of birds. Some suppliers sell seed types to suit winter and summer feeding.*

Seeds and grains: *Seeds are the staple diet of many species, while grains tend to be the winter diet of woodland and farmland birds.*

Fat: *Specially designed food bars, containing insects, suet and other animal fats, are excellent energy-providers, especially in winter.*

Fruit: *Fresh fruit is popular with many birds. Apples, oranges, grapes, pears, plums and peaches are all a welcome addition to the diet.*

Leftovers: *Food scraps – bread, cooked rice, lentils, cheese and dog food – provide a good supplementary diet for a wide variety of bird species.*

NESTING AND NESTBOXES

Apart from providing a regular supply of food and water, the next best thing you can do for your garden birds is to provide safe places to nest. Planting a good variety of trees, bushes and shrubs will provide natural nest sites, but you can help even further by putting up nestboxes. Nestboxes are simply an artificial way of creating a nest site for birds that normally nest in crevices or holes in trees.

Natural nest sites are in relatively short supply, and competition means that many birds fail to find a place to nest. By designing and building nestboxes – and mounting them on buildings or trees correctly (positioning is important) – we are offering a safe and convenient, much-needed alternative.

Nestboxes also look attractive, especially if you make them yourself and spend time and trouble at all stages. The boxes described in the following projects are carefully designed and easy on the eye – great fun to make and good for the birds.

Nestbox designs

Nestboxes come in all shapes and sizes (see Part 3). An open-fronted box is suitable for species such as the robin. A box with a small entrance hole will accommodate titmice, sparrows, and similar species. Other designs include a chimney box (made from a hollowed-out piece of wood) for owls, and a wedge-shaped box for Brown Creepers.

Once you've made your nestbox, it must be sited in the best place to attract birds. It will also need yearly maintenance to keep it in good condition.

FOUR TYPES OF NESTBOX

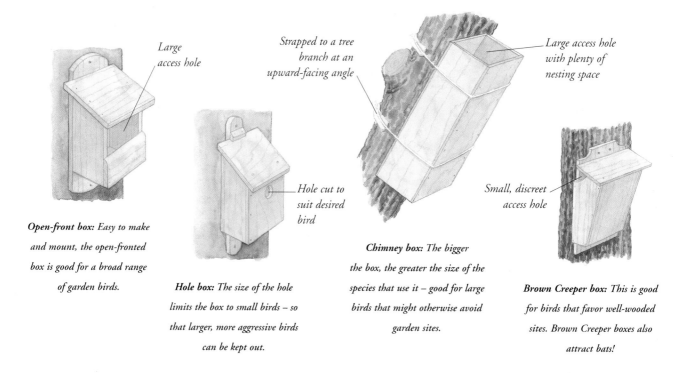

Large access hole

Strapped to a tree branch at an upward-facing angle

Large access hole with plenty of nesting space

Hole cut to suit desired bird

Small, discreet access hole

Open-front box: Easy to make and mount, the open-fronted box is good for a broad range of garden birds.

Hole box: The size of the hole limits the box to small birds – so that larger, more aggressive birds can be kept out.

Chimney box: The bigger the box, the greater the size of the species that use it – good for large birds that might otherwise avoid garden sites.

Brown Creeper box: This is good for birds that favor well-wooded sites. Brown Creeper boxes also attract bats!

Nestbox maintenance

Once the breeding season begins, it is best to leave the box well alone, as too frequent inspections can cause the parent birds to desert. However, once the eggs are being incubated you may make the occasional quick check – just to make sure that all is well.

After the chicks have fledged and left the nest, give the box a good clean, removing any old nesting material and scrubbing with soap and hot water.

With luck, a well-considered, beautifully made and carefully positioned box will provide an excellent home for birds year after year, and give you and your family hours of pleasure watching their breeding activities.

Nestboxes should be sited carefully: the box on the left is too low and in full glare of the sun, so would not be suitable for nesting birds.

Siting a nestbox

A nestbox should always be fixed to a firm base: either a wall, tree, fence or post. Height is not critical, but it should normally be at least 5 feet above the ground. Don't put the box too high, or you will be unable to reach it easily for maintenance.

Direction is important: baby birds can fry in hot sunshine, so it's best to site the box in the shade, preferably facing in any direction between north-east and south-east. Try to keep the box away from thick foliage or other places that would make it easy for predators to gain entry. Don't put boxes too close to each other, as birds will fight other birds entering their territory.

PESTS AND PREDATORS

I*t can sometimes seem as if your garden is a battleground between squabbling birds, pesky squirrels and murderous cats. In many ways that's a fair picture: nature truly is "red in tooth and claw", even within the cozy confines of the garden, when food is at stake. If we provide a fast-food restaurant and hotel for the birds, we shouldn't be surprised if less welcome visitors abuse our hospitality.*

PESTS

Let's start with garden pests such as aphids, slugs and caterpillars, the bane of many a gardener's life. Here you have two choices: either smother your plants with pesticides and slug killer, or try a less aggressive approach, encouraging natural predators such as ladybirds, frogs and toads into the garden. Remember that birds themselves help get rid of pests: Song Thrushes make short work of slugs, while many species of bird will take caterpillars, especially during the breeding season.

If you do decide to use sprays and chemicals, then at least try to use the more eco-friendly varieties, obtainable from reputable garden centers.

Squirrels can make short work of traditional bird feeders, ripping them apart to get to the contents. One solution is to use squirrel-proof feeders.

Many birds will eat the slugs and snails that can wipe out a vegetable crop.

A wildlife garden should always have room for beneficial insects. These seven-spot ladybirds are hibernating inside the seedhead of this plant.

Larger pests include rats and mice, which feast on spilled food from feeders and bird tables, making it essential that you clean up as often as possible. But perhaps the most annoying mammal of all is the one known affectionately as the "American tree rat" – the squirrel.

Squirrels are among the most agile, acrobatic and ingenious of all animals, and are particularly partial to peanuts. One way to foil their efforts is to construct a squirrel-proof feeder (see page 50), which lets the smaller birds in while keeping the squirrels at bay. Nestboxes should also be protected, as far as possible, from attack by marauding squirrels, which are always on the lookout for a tasty snack of eggs or chicks.

CATS

The world seems to be divided into two camps: people who love cats, and people who don't. Oddly, the first camp also includes many millions of people who love birds. These kind souls often encourage birds to come into their garden for food and shelter where they are in danger of becoming dinner for their own pet cat!

Cats are responsible for countless millions of bird deaths each year – so how do you protect the birds that you are attracting to your own garden? Well, if you don't like cats, you can buy a device which emits a high-pitched sound unbearable to a cat's ears which will keep them out of your garden area. But if you or your neighbor owns a cat, this may not be a practical option. Bells round a cat's neck are fairly ineffective, though perhaps a really large, loud one will give some warning.

Generally, you must remember to site your bird feeders and bird baths in a relatively open space, so that cats are not able to creep up easily on birds while they are feeding or bathing. Nestboxes should be fairly safe, but make sure that they are not sited too near the ground or close to convenient branches if fixed to a tree.

BIRD PREDATORS

A final word on bird predators such as jays, magpies and sparrow hawks. Many people consider these to be the real villains of the bird world: they are ruthless predators that kill millions of songbirds. Although these species do kill smaller birds, we should remember that this is their purpose in life. Predators and prey have a balanced relationship, in which numbers of the latter generally regulate populations of the former.

There are many reasons why bird predators have increased in recent years, not least the welcome reduction in shooting and the banning of pesticides such as DDT. In some ways, we are responsible for attracting these birds into our gardens: after all, by providing plenty of food we attract artificially high concentrations of small birds, which make easy pickings for predators. We must also remember that most songbirds will die before they reach a year old, and falling prey to a sparrow hawk is at least a quick and natural way to die – unlike being tormented by a well-fed domestic cat. So you can experience the spectacle of one of the bird world's greatest hunters without guilt.

There are cat lovers and there are bird lovers.
I would reckon that this fat cat is a bird lover!

Part 2

MATERIALS, TOOLS AND TECHNIQUES

uilding birdhouses, boxes and feeders from wood is a
B *rewarding and therapeutic activity… but only, it must
be said, if you are using the appropriate tools, materials and
techniques. It doesn't matter if you only have a small working
area, as long as you have a workbench and a few carefully
selected tools. Whether you're an expert or a novice, this
section will show you the way.*

MATERIALS

While all manner of materials could undoubtedly be used to build bird houses and feeders – such as plastics, metal or concrete – we prefer to use wood from sustainable sources in conjunction with acrylic paint and basic hardware. We feel that these materials are, to a great extent, "green" – non-toxic, non-polluting, biodegradable and easy to work with – altogether man- and bird-friendly.

SOME OF THE MATERIALS YOU WILL NEED

Oak
Rough-sawn with bark edges

Oak
Rough-sawn with one bark face

Pine
Fence stake

Cherry
Log with the bark intact

Basswood
Rough-sawn plank

Cherry
Planed plank

Plywood
Best quality, exterior grade

Pine
Rough-sawn plank

Feather-edge board
Tapered-section, rough-sawn pine

Stick
Wood with the bark intact

Pole
Wood with the bark removed

Rattan
Natural basket-weaving fibre

Mesh
Galvanized wire square mesh

Threaded rod
Zinc coated, with nut and washer

Pine
Planed square-section

Dowel
Round-section wood

Most children enjoy helping to build birdhouses and feeders – not only are they fascinated by the prospect of mini houses and their bird visitors, but they also like being involved in the construction process. While it is vital that you encourage their interest, you must also be very aware of safety. Make sure they wear safety glasses and a dust-mask when necessary. If you are going to show them how to hammer in nails, saw wood, or whatever, then guide them through it on a one-to-one basis. Always supervise children in the workshop, and do any tasks involving power tools yourself. Never try to supervise more than two children at a time.

LUMBER

We always advocate using exterior-grade plywood and various easy-to-find, sustainable native woods – cherry, oak, ash and pine – either as rough-sawn planks, or as in-bark (barky) slab wood. The best source for rough-sawn planks and barky wood is the sort of operation that sells fence posts, bean poles, garden timber and logs. The wood is usually sold "as is" – meaning you turn up, look the wood over, and choose the piece that suits. You will often find that the supplier directs you to a stack of heavy, wet wood piled high, so wear heavy footwear and old clothes, and take thick gloves to protect your hands. Remember that when buying barky wood, the wider the slab, the thicker the piece. Also, as barky wood is the first slice from the log, it will be wildly waney-edged (the uncut edge of the board will be curved). Study the working drawings, and be ready to modify the projects to suit the available wood.

HARDWARE

While all the projects demand exterior-grade screws and nails – so, in theory, you could use brass or aluminum – our preferred choice is steel, either plain or galvanized. The mix of rough-sawn wood, barky green slab wood, painted and sanded plywood, dully gleaming galvanized nails, and wood streaked with rust, all makes for an aesthetically pleasing whole. As to whether or not you decide to use flat-headed nails, or nails with heads that can be driven below the surface, it really depends on your choice of wood. If you feel that the wood is likely to split, or the bark will slip off, then flat-headed nails are best. Screws can be either slot-headed or cross-headed, as long as the length and diameter fit the bill.

When using wire mesh, we always choose a good-quality galvanized square-grid mesh, on the grounds that it is easy to work and structurally strong in its own right. If the fixings fail, then the rigid gridded mesh usually stays put much better than woven mesh.

A selection of the pins, nails, staples and screws needed for making the projects, is shown above: 1. Panel nail, bright steel, 1½ in; 2. Panel nail, bright steel, ¾ in; 3. Panel nail, bright steel, 1 in; 4. Round-headed nail, bright steel, 2¼ in; 5. Staple, galvanized, 18 mm or ¾ in; 6. Flat-headed nail, galvanized, 1½ in; 7. Slot-headed screw, zinc coated, 1 in; 8. Cross-headed screw, zinc coated, 1 in; 9. Slot-headed screw, zinc coated, ½ in; 10. Slot-headed screw, bright steel, ¾ in.

PAINTS AND GLUES

The primary concern is that the paints and glues should be non-polluting, low-odor and non-toxic. We have opted for using water-based acrylic paints, varnishes and glues, which can be used without wearing a face-mask. The brushes are easy to wash, and most importantly of all, these materials are safe for the birds. Apart from using minute amounts of artist's oil paint, we avoid petrochemical paints.

TOOLS AND TECHNIQUES

These projects will supply you with lots of juicy woodworking tasks – sawing, nailing, sanding, painting, and so on – all of which are enjoyable. But the whole construction process is so much more of a pleasure when you use the correct tools for the job, and have a clear understanding of the basic techniques.

MEASURING AND MARKING

Pencils

Box rule

Straight-edge (and ruler)

Dividers

Compass

Compass and dividers

Though a compass is primarily used for scribing out circles, while dividers are used for reading and transferring measurements, both tools are, to a great extent, interchangeable. We tend to use a compass for setting out circles on plywood and doing the more delicate working drawings. We prefer to use dividers for transferring measurements and drawing circles on rough-sawn wood – simply because they are more robust and can survive the wear and tear of woodworking.

Try square

Engineer's adjustable square

Steel tape measure

Pencil, ruler, straight-edge and tape measure

For all woodwork that starts with measurements and drawn lines, you will need a selection of pencils, a ruler, a straight-edge, and a measuring tape. A good set-up would include hard and soft pencils for drawing directly on to the wood, a box rule for small, precise measurements, a foot-long steel rule that doubles up as a straight-edge, and a steel tape measure for measurements greater than a foot. Because products come from all over the world, it's a good idea to use rulers that combine both metric and imperial gradations.

Square

Woodwork is an ongoing procedure of testing that lines and edges are at right angles to each other. If you need to set out a corner, or check that one edge is true to another, then you must use a square. While a traditional steel and wood try square can be used for most tasks, an all-metal engineer's adjustable square can be used both for straightforward squaring, and for drawing out all the angles through to 180 degrees. So if you are going to purchase a square, go for an engineer's square with a dual protractor head and a square head.

SAWING

Hand saw

Back saw

Bar clamp

Hand saw and back saw

Hand saw teeth can vary in fineness. Coarser teeth are designed to cut in the direction of the grain (down the length of a plank), while finer teeth are designed to cut at right angles to the run of the grain (across the width of a plank). If you intend to work with green slab wood, then you will need a saw with "universal" teeth. Once the wood has been sawn to size with the hand saw, you will need to use a back saw to make the finer cuts that are required for the project. We use a tenon saw for general bench work, and a gents saw for thin-section wood. Both these back saws are used along with a traditional bench, vice, bar clamp and/or portable patent trestle vice.

Bandsaw

The bandsaw is the perfect tool for cutting curves in thick-section wood. You can fit the saw with different sizes and grades of blade – a fine-toothed narrow blade for tight curves in thin-section wood, and a heavy-toothed wide blade for broader curves in thick-section wood. A small, two-wheeled bench-top

Bandsaw

machine is perfectly adequate for all the projects in this book. The wood is held down on the cutting table and maneuvered so that the blade is presented with the line of cut. The primary safety rule is to always keep your fingers away from the front of the blade. If you have doubts, use a push-stick to advance the wood.

Scroll saw

While a bandsaw is used for cutting generous curves in thick-section wood, the scroll saw (sometimes called a jigsaw or fretsaw) is used for cutting intricate

Scroll saw

curves in thin-section wood. The scroll saw is as safe as a machine can be. The very worst that you can do is scratch your fingers. The wood is held down firmly on the table and fed towards the jiggling blade. If you like fine, fretted curves, and you are working in a limited space, then the scroll saw is ideal.

Bow saw

Hacksaw

Bow saw and hacksaw

Generally, a bow saw is not really considered to be a woodworking tool, but it is perfect for cutting damp, green barky wood. We use two very ordinary workaday saws – a large one for the rough task of cutting the wood into manageable lengths, and a smaller, easy-to-handle saw for little cuts. These saws can be purchased from home improvement stores. You will also need a small hacksaw for cutting bolts and threaded rod.

SAFETY TIP – SAWDUST

Fine wood dust is not only bad for the lungs, eyes and skin, it is also a fire risk. If you are working with dust-making machines, such as the bandsaw and scroll saw, wear a dust-mask, and control the dust by using a vacuum system. Working outdoors is a healthy option.

Dust-mask

CARVING

**Gouge, mallet, adze,
V-section tool and paring chisel**

Gouges are designed to make a curved, scooping cut – appearing as a "U" or "C" in cross-section. The terms "straight", "bent", "curved" and "spoon" describe the shape of the blade along its length. Generally, straight gouges are used for surface work, while bent, curved and

Straight gouge

Spoon gouge

Curved gouge

Adze

Mallet

V-section tool

Paring chisel

spoon gouges are used for scooping out holes. The piece of work is clamped to the bench – for this a sash clamp is ideal – and the gouge is used with or without a wooden mallet. The adze is used like an axe, and is good for carving hollows. The V-section tool cuts a furrow, while a paring chisel is designed to make skimming cuts.

Drawknife

Knife

Small penknife

Knives and drawknives

A knife is a wonderful tool for all the trimming tasks involved in building bird houses and feeders. We use a small penknife for whittling pegs and for delicate shaping, and a larger knife for cutting rods and poles.

A drawknife is a two-handled knife that is used for tasks such as skinning poles and shaping rods. The work-piece is held secure in the vice or clamp, while the drawknife is held in both hands and worked with a pulling, slicing stroke.

SAFETY TIP – KNIVES

Children tend to be fascinated by knives. Always keep knives in a locked cupboard and show the children how to use them when they are old enough.

DRILLING

Hand-held power drill

Clamp

Bench drill press

Brace

Pinion drill

Power drills

Ideally you should have two power-operated drills: a good-size bench drill press for large-diameter holes in component parts, and a hand-held drill for all the smaller holes that you need to make for nails, screws and bolts. If you do decide to use a hand-held power drill to bore large-diameter holes, you must secure the workpiece with clamps.

Hand drills

We have two hand drills: a traditional brace, and a small "egg beater-type" single-pinion drill. The brace is particularly useful for drilling deep, wide holes in unseasoned green wood, while the pinion drill is great for small-diameter holes in plywood and thin-section wood – when you can't be bothered to get out the electric drill.

Auger, general purpose and forstner bits

We use forstner bits in the drill press, a mix of forstner and general purpose bits in the electric drill, auger bits in the brace, and small general purpose bits in the pinion drill. Forstner bits are ideal for smooth-sided, flat-bottomed, large-diameter holes, and for getting rid of waste when carving.

Auger bit   *General purpose bits*   *Forstner bit*

ASSEMBLING

Screwdriver

Screws, screwdrivers and threaded rod

Screws (see page 21) and threaded rod (see page 20) are invaluable. We use screws rather than pins for fixing plywood when we require greater strength. Threaded rod is good for situations where you need bolts of a non-standard length: all you do is cut the threaded rod to length, and use it in conjunction with washers and nuts. Threaded rod comes in various lengths and diameters. You will need a range of screwdrivers to fit your chosen screws, and a hacksaw to cut the threaded rod to length.

Long-nose pliers

Claw hammer   *Pin hammer*   *Wire snips*

Nails, panel nails, hammers and pliers

We favor using a mix of panel nails, steel nails and galvanized nails (see page 21): panel nails for thin-section wood and plywood, steel nails for thick-section green wood, and galvanized nails for just about everything else. You will need two hammers: a good-size claw hammer for driving in and drawing out large nails, and a pin hammer for knocking in small nails and pins accurately.

To assist nailing and to straighten and extract nails, you will need a pair of long-nose pliers; for cutting wire mesh, a pair of wire snips is required.

Glue

Plywood is best fixed with glue and panel nails. We use exterior-grade PVA wood glue, which is tough and flexible, and as far as we know, does not give off vapors that are harmful to birds. Beware of epoxy glues, and glues that are petroleum based. It is a good idea to follow your nose – if a glue has a strong smell, birds will not like it.

SANDING AND PAINTING

Sandpaper and sanding blocks

Sanding is the technique of using graded abrasives to cut back a rough surface to a smooth finish. There are all manner of abrasives, but the projects in this book are best worked with a traditional sandpaper or glasspaper. The paper can either be folded (so that you can reach into tight corners) or it can be wrapped around a sanding block (in order to sand large, flat surfaces).

Sandpaper

Sanding block

Paints and finishes

We prefer to use water-based acrylics, applied in thin coats to enhance the character of the underlying wood. The wood must be sanded down to a smooth finish before brushing on the paint. When it is dry, you can rub through the paint to achieve a distressed effect. Give the finished project a coat of water-based exterior matte or gloss varnish.

Paintbrush

MOUNTING METHODS

Bird houses and feeders need to be securely mounted on a tree, building, fence, wall or a freestanding pole. Look for a sheltered site (if on a building, make sure the bird house will not damage it), where the birds will be safe from predators. Ensure that the position does not present any hazards for birds or bird-watchers.

MOUNTING ON POLES

Square of wood to link the feeder to the post

The post needs to be at least 5 ft long

Post slots into fence post spike

A brace to spread the load and strengthen the structure

Base is fixed to the ground with pegs

Use screws instead of nails for additional strength

The best option is to have four brace pieces

End of post is sharpened

Fence post with metal socket: *The socket is hammered into the ground, and the post is screwed or bolted into place.*

Freestanding bracket construction: *For additional support on a windy site, the stand is secured to the ground with tent pegs.*

Rustic post: *Quick to make and easy to replace, this design will blend into the fabric of the garden.*

Depending on the type and size of the bird house or feeder, it may be mounted on a freestanding pole. A pole can be banged or dug into the ground, slotted into a special metal fence post spike, or supported on its own bracketed base. The bracketed base gives you the option of easily repositioning the whole thing at a later date, but it does make for a lot more work. Banging the pole into the ground is perhaps the simplest method, but the bottom of the pole is likely to rot and decay. The metal fence spike will provide a stable structure, but you do have to consider buried electric cables, gas or water pipes. We prefer to hammer the pole straight into the ground – it's quick, and to our mind, the eventual rot and decay are all part and parcel of the natural "green" garden.

MOUNTING NESTBOXES ON BUILDINGS

Concrete or brick — *Nestbox* — *Expanding bolt attaching*

Attaching for concrete: *Use special bolts. Good for mounting heavy boxes (also for brick).*

Brick — *Nestbox* — *Plastic plug* — *Screw*

Attaching for brick: *Use a screw and plug. Avoid attaching into the mortar coursing.*

Screw and plastic wall plug attaching

Mount box at least 5 ¾ ft from the ground

Nestbox mounted on a brick wall: *For additional strength – and to stop the box tilting – use two attachings.*

Metal attaching plates provide extra support

Screw attaching (no plug needed)

Dovecote mounted on a wooden wall: *For heavy boxes, use metal attaching plates screwed to the back of the structure.*

Many birds favor boxes mounted on buildings – no doubt their bird sense tells them that buildings are, in many ways, akin to muddy banks or cliff faces. You need to take into account what is best for the building, and what is best for the birds. The best type of attaching method is to use screws and anchors, or small expanding bolts. It's much better to drill into the brick than the mortar, as it does less damage to the building, and is more secure for the box. Pick a spot that is away from windows, rainwater downpipes, tree branches and fences – you don't want rain dribbling into the box, or to allow cats and squirrels to reach the box by walking along a branch or fence. On no account drill holes into the roof overhang, as this might have been made of asbestos cement.

MOUNTING ON TREES

Pad of plastic to protect tree

Galvanized wire strap

Mounting a chimney box: *Hang the box under a branch (facing upwards) to disguise it from predators.*

Nailed to tree trunk

Angled away from wind and rain

Mounting an open-front box: *Position the box so that the opening is sheltered from the worst of the weather.*

Plastic pad

Rope, wire or chain

Mounting a hanging feeder: *The feeder is suspended from a substantial tree branch at a height that is easy to reach.*

Find a suitable mature tree, walk around it and try to work out which direction the prevailing weather comes from. Ideally, the box needs to be sited to face away from the wind and rain. Take into consideration the recommended box height for the birds you want to attract, and pick a spot that is safe from cats and squirrels. The box can be nailed, screwed or wired into place. Make sure it is stable, and avoid damaging the tree as much as possible. Some feeders can of course be suspended from a branch on a rope or wire.

Part 3

THE PROJECTS

Woodworking is a great activity in its own right – an exciting journey into the wonderful world of sawing, carving and drilling – and what better at the end of it all, than to have made a birdhouse or feeder? You and your family will be able to watch young birds being fed, chickadees getting up to their noisy antics – you will have created an engaging focal point in the garden. Even if you are more of a bird enthusiast than a woodworker, our carefully structured step-by-step projects will guide you to success.

NATURAL LOG TITMOUSE BOX

This log nesting box – sometimes known as the "Berlepsch" log box – is, without doubt, the greenest of titmouse boxes. Designed in the last quarter of the nineteenth century by the eccentric German landowner Baron Von Berlepsch, the whole idea of the box is to create (as near as possible) an exact replica of a natural nesting cavity. It was first marketed in England by the Royal Society for the Protection of Birds.

DESIGN NOTES

The design is beautiful in its simplicity – just a hollowed-out log, a disc of wood for the base plug, a piece of plywood for the back board, a whittled peg and a few holes – and you have the ultimate in eco-friendly nest-boxes. If you like the notion of a titmouse box that will be at one with the trees, and if you enjoy basic wood-carving, then this is the project to make.

We selected a cherry log for the box – because it carves easily and looks good – but you can use any wood that takes your fancy, if it is reasonably straight-grained, easy to carve, and will blend in with the site.

Materials

- Cherry log, 15 in long and about 7⅞ in in diameter (A)
- Exterior plywood, 15 in long, ⅜ in thick and 6¾ in wide (B)
- Pine, 7⅞ in long, 1¾ in thick and 7⅞ in wide (C)
- Pine, 9 in long, 1 in thick and 1½ in wide (D)
- Panel nails, 1 in
- Nail for fixing, 3¼ in

Tools

- Workbench with vice
- Pencil and ruler
- Small axe and chopping log
- Sash clamp
- Straight gouges, ½ in and 1 in wide
- Electric drill
- Bench drill press
- Forstner drill bits, ⅜ in, ½ in and 1 in
- Bent gouge, 1½ in wide
- Mallet
- Pin and claw hammers
- Penknife

A BIRD-FRIENDLY BOX

Many of our common garden birds nest in holes in trees, where eggs and chicks are safer from most common predators. With a shortage of suitable natural nest sites, this basic "titmouse box" is an essential feature of every bird-friendly garden.

The most likely occupants are titmice, although depending on the location, House and Tree Sparrows, or even nuthatches and chickadees may take advantage of a ready-made home.

Site your nestbox during autumn or winter, to allow the birds to get used to its presence. The best place is on a fence or wall facing from north-east to south-east, to avoid strong sunlight, and between 5 and 16 feet above the ground. It is also useful to tilt the front of the nestbox downwards a little, to create an overhang that keeps out the rain. For more information, the Office of Migratory Bird Management run by the U.S. Fish and Wildlife Service has an internet site with pamphlets on backyard birding and nest boxes. Visit http://migratorybirds.fws.gov.

Once the birds have chosen to nest, there will be a period of frenetic activity, as they go to and fro with nesting material. Once egg-laying begins, things go quiet, though during incubation the male will bring food for the female. After hatching, the activity begins again, until a couple of weeks later the chicks finally leave the nest and face the outside world.

Step 1: Axing the log

Step 2: Carving the roof slope

Step 3: Drilling out the waste

Step 4: Gouging the hollow

Step 5: Fitting the base plug

Step 6: Fitting the back board

Step 7: Drilling the access hole

Step 8: Whittling the peg

CONSTRUCTION DETAILS FOR THE NATURAL LOG TITMOUSE BOX

7⅞ in

⅜ in
fixing hole

15 in

7⅞ in

1 in access hole
for the titmouse

A

D

FRONT VIEW

B

SIDE VIEW

Carved edge to
the access hole

¾ in thick

1¾ in thick

CROSS-
SECTION

Peg holds base
plug in place

PLAN VIEW

Inside of log
is carved out

C

Removable base
plug is a snug fit

EXPLODED VIEW

HOW TO MAKE THE PROJECT

Step 1: Axing the log Having used a pencil and ruler to set out the length of the log (A), use the axe to work the back of the log to a flat finish about 6¾ inches wide.

Step 2: Carving the roof slope Support the end of the log against the sash clamp and use the straight gouges to carve the top of the log into a gentle slope.

Step 3: Drilling out the waste Set the log front face-down on the bench and use the drill and the 1 inch forstner bit to clear the bulk of the waste.

Step 4: Gouging the hollow Clamp the workpiece in the vice and use the bent gouge to scoop out the remaining waste. Aim for a hollow 6½ inches in diameter.

Step 5: Fitting the base plug Trim the base plug (C) to snugly fit the hollow. Tap it into place with the mallet.

Step 6: Fitting the back board Cut the plywood board (B) to fit the back of the log and fix with the panel nails.

Step 7: Drilling the access hole Establish a hole center 7⅞ inches up from the base of the box, and use the 1 inch forstner drill bit (with the drill press) to bore the access hole through into the hollow.

Step 8: Whittling the peg Drill a hole ½ inch in diameter across the width of the log, through the wall thickness and through the base plug. Whittle a peg (D) for this hole. Drill an ⅜ inch hole at the top of the box.

MOUNTING
Select a suitable site on a fence, wall or stout tree, and position the box 5 to 16 feet above the ground. Angle the entrance hole away from strong sunlight and the prevailing winds, and nail the box firmly in place.

STANDARD OPEN-FRONT BOX

This traditional open-front design draws its inspiration from the type of Edwardian mailbox that was often hung in the porch of an English country house. Its fancy stepped profile, generous angled roof, and subtle colorwashed finish will enhance your garden. The carefully thought-out dimensions and structure of this box will attract birds such as robins and flycatchers.

DESIGN NOTES

If you have been looking for an open-front box for your garden, but you have been somewhat put off by the ill-considered, plywood-and-plastic bird houses that are usually sold, then this project is tailor-made for you. The six-board design is wonderfully easy to make. All the boards are both glued and nailed – for extra strength and to keep out the weather – and the whole work is made from rough-sawn cherry, making it a choice project for the beginner who has a yen for something that is a little bit special.

Materials

- Cherry, 22 in long, ⅝ in thick and 7⅞ in wide (A)
- 2 x pieces cherry, 16 in long, ⅝ in thick and 5⅝ in wide (B)
- Cherry, 9 in long, ⅝ in thick and 7¾ in wide (C)
- Cherry, 5⅜ in long, ⅝ in thick and 6½ in wide (D)
- Cherry, 7⅞ in long, ⅝ in thick and 3¾ in wide (E)
- Exterior-grade PVA wood glue
- Panel nails, 1½ in
- Acrylic paint, pale green
- Clear exterior-quality varnish
- Screws, 2 x 2 in

Tools

- Workbench with vice
- Pencil, ruler and compass
- Engineer's square
- Penknife
- Scroll saw fitted with a fine blade
- Electric drill
- Bench drill press
- Forstner drill bits, ⅞ in and 1 in
- Sandpaper and sanding block
- Pin hammer
- Small paintbrush
- Screwdriver

A VERSATILE BOX

Some species of bird, including robins and flycatchers, prefer to make a nest in a crevice, or build a cup-shaped nest in a suitable nook or cranny. For them, the best nestbox design is one with an open front.

The nice thing about this design is that you don't have to be too accurate with your measurements – after all, natural crevices aren't always perfectly shaped! Another advantage is that you can easily inspect the box and its contents, enabling you to see the eggs and chicks – but don't spend too long looking, or you might cause the birds to desert.

The only drawback is that this kind of nestbox leaves the occupants very vulnerable to predation, especially from jays, magpies and cats.

As with the titmouse box, choose a sheltered site, where the birds are protected from prevailing wind, rain and direct sunlight. Placing the box amongst some foliage – for example a climbing plant such as a clematis, can provide shelter and some protection against intruders. Also, keep the box away from bird tables and feeders as the presence of feeding birds nearby may deter potential occupants from nesting.

Step 1: Setting out the design

Step 2: Using the scroll saw

Step 3: Drilling out the mounting holes

Step 4: Fitting together

Step 5: Applying the colorwash

Step 6: Sanding and finishing

CONSTRUCTION DETAILS FOR THE OPEN-FRONT BOX

CROSS-SECTION

FRONT VIEW

SIDE VIEW

EXPLODED VIEW

PLAN VIEW

HOW TO MAKE THE PROJECT

Step 1: Setting out the design Set out the back board (A) with the ruler and engineer's square. To mark out the decorative half-circle on both ends, fix the compass to a radius of 1½ inches, spike the point on the center-line, 1½ inches in from the end of the board, and draw the half-circle. Mark out the steps with the penknife.

Step 2: Using the scroll saw Cut out the half-circle and steps on the back board (A). Cut out the other pieces (B, C, D and E). Advance the workpiece at a steady pace, with the cutting line slightly to the waste side of the drawn line.

Step 3: Drilling out the mounting holes Using the 1 inch forstner bit and the drill press, drill to a depth of about ⁵⁄₁₆ inch – half the thickness of the back board (A). Change to the ⅜ inch bit and continue to drill right through the board. Do this on both ends of the board.

Step 4: Fitting together Sand down the edges of all the pieces to a smooth, square finish. Apply the glue to all mating faces, and join. Fix with the panel nails.

Step 5: Applying the colorwash Dilute the acrylic paint with water and brush on repeated coats until you have an attractive density of color.

Step 6: Sanding and finishing Use the sandpaper to rub away areas of the paint to reveal the grain and create a worn appearance. Varnish.

MOUNTING

Spend time selecting a suitable site about 5 to 16 feet above the ground – it might be on a wooden shed, a wall, or a limb or fork of a stout tree. Position the box to face away from the prevailing wind and rain, and screw it firmly in place.

BARK BROWN CREEPER BOX

*T*he Brown Creeper box is a winner on many counts. The bark is left intact so that the box is perfectly camouflaged; it is made from easy-to-work green wood; the interior surfaces are rough-sawn and gouge-textured, providing good footholds for the nestlings; and the whole project can be assembled easily and quickly.

DESIGN NOTES

The clever thing about this design is the way the back slab is cut and worked, so that the front and roof slabs notch together allowing the rain to run down and off the box without entering it. The bark on the front of the box runs from top to bottom, making it almost invisible when it is mounted on a tree. Perhaps most importantly of all, in view of the concerns about declining wood resources, the design uses first-cut sawmill wood that would otherwise be wasted.

When you are searching for wood, do your best to select sound slabs of hardwood with the bark still firmly attached. If the wood is in any way faulted – long splits, spongy areas, pierced with large insect holes – then look around for another piece.

Materials

(All thickness measurements are necessarily average, with some slabs being considerably thicker in part.)

- Sawn oak, 23⅝ in long, 1⅞6 in thick and 6¼ in wide (A)
- Sawn oak, 10⅝ in long, 1 in thick and 8 in wide (B)
- 2 x pieces sawn oak, 10⅝ in long, 1 in thick and 5⅞ in wide (C)
- Sawn oak, 7⅞6 in long, 1 in thick and 9½ in wide (D)

- Galvanized nails, 2 in
- 2 x galvanized nails, 3¼ in

Tools

- Workbench with vice
- Pencil, ruler, square and dividers
- Small bandsaw
- Small log saw
- Straight gouge, 1⅛6 in wide
- Mallet
- Pin and claw hammers

BROWN CREEPER HOME

*T*he Brown Creeper is one of our most endearing little birds, and also one of the easiest to overlook. As the name suggests, Brown Creepers spend most of their lives creeping up tree trunks, and along branches, in search of food – tiny insects and spiders – which they lift from beneath the bark with their narrow, decurved bill. Their dull brown plumage and creeping habit make this bird difficult to see.

Brown Creepers are one of the most sedentary of birds, and are highly vulnerable during prolonged spells of icy weather, especially when "glazed frosts" cover twigs and branches with a thin layer of ice.

They are woodland birds, so are not frequent visitors to most gardens. However, if you have a large garden in the country it is well worth considering the intriguing design of this nestbox. You could also erect the box in nearby woodland, provided that you obtain permission from the owner first.

The idea of this box is to make it look as much like the natural nesting site of the Brown Creeper as possible. Brown Creepers generally nest in tiny cracks and crevices beneath the bark, using twigs, stems, roots and bark – the nest is often concealed behind a curtain of ivy. They usually lay five or six pale, slightly spotted eggs.

As with all nestboxes, take special care when siting the Brown Creeper box, as a fall from a tree can be dangerous. Use a sturdy ladder and ask a partner to hold it steady while you fix the box.

Step 1: Setting out the wood

Step 2: Using the bandsaw

Step 3: Using the log saw

Step 4: Cutting the back board notches

Step 5: Fitting the side boards

Step 6: Putting together

CONSTRUCTION DETAILS FOR THE BARK BROWN CREEPER BOX

CROSS-
SECTION

FRONT VIEW

SIDE VIEW

EXPLODED VIEW

2¼ in radius

Top edge
is carved

Bark surfaces
face outwards

8 in
6¼ in

7⁷⁄₁₆ in
5¼ in
10⅜ in

23⅜ in
7⅜ in
2¼ in
2⁷⁄₁₆ in

9⅜ in

PLAN VIEW

A

C

D

B

C

HOW TO MAKE THE PROJECT

Step 1: Setting out the wood Use the pencil, ruler, square and dividers to set out the measurements on the sawn face of the wood. Do your best to avoid deep knot-holes, twisted grain and splits.

Step 2: Using the bandsaw Cut out the pieces. Bearing in mind that you will have to cut the wood with the bark face on the underside (consequently the blade will snatch), you must be extra careful to keep your fingers well away from the front of the blade. You will need help with the larger boards.

Step 3: Using the bow saw Run the two stop-cut notches halfway through the 1⁷⁄₁₆ inches thickness of the back board (A). Aim to finish up with the bottom of the cuts parallel to the back sawn face of the wood.

Step 4: Cutting the back board notches Use the mallet and gouge to remove the waste between the two stop-cut notches. Hold the gouge at a low angle and work from center through to end – so that the length of the gouge stroke is controlled by the stop-cut. Clear the waste from one end, then turn the wood around and repeat the procedure for the other end.

Step 5: Fitting the side boards Have a trial dry-run so that you know how the project comes together, and then nail the two side boards (C) firmly in place on the back board, using the pin hammer and the 2 inch nails.

Step 6: Putting together When you are satisfied with the stability and appearance of the structure, go over the whole box, fixing with additional nails.

MOUNTING

Choose a suitable tree, and position the box about 8 to 16 feet above the ground, with the side entrance holes in a sheltered spot away from strong sunlight. Using the claw hammer, fix firmly in place with the 3¼ inch nails at the top and bottom.

OWL CHIMNEY BOX

For many bird lovers, the very thought of having owls in the garden tops the excitement scale. For the chance to watch owls swooping to rest, "twit-twooing" to each other, the mother owl bringing food for her young and chicks learning to fly, – this box is a must-have!

DESIGN NOTES

In many ways, this design is delightful in its simplicity – not much more than five in-bark slabs nailed together to make a box. But fresh-sawn green wood is damp, difficult to saw up, subject to faults, and heavy. The best way to deal with it is to use large-toothed saws and oil the blades, to pre-drill nail holes, and to get help with lifting.

As green wood tends to be cheap, you can even make a mock-up version first, to iron out potential problems. If you are a fan of large-scale, instant-result woodwork, you will enjoy this project.

Materials

(All thickness measurements are necessarily average, with some slabs being considerably thicker in part.)

- Sawn oak, 32¼ in long, 2⅜ in thick and 11 in wide (A)
- 2 x pieces sawn oak, 26¾ in long, 2¼ in thick and 6½ in wide (B)
- Sawn oak, 26¾ in long, 2¼ in thick and 8 in wide (C)
- Sawn oak, 6½ in long, 2⅜ in thick and 6½ in wide (D)
- Vegetable oil
- Galvanized nails, 3¼ in
- Galvanized wire

Tools

- Workbench with vice, bar clamp and bench stop
- Pencil, ruler, straight-edge and square
- Hand saw
- Bow saw
- Straight gouge, 1 in wide
- Mallet
- Electric drill
- General purpose drill bit, ⁵⁄₁₆ in
- Claw hammer

HUNTERS IN YOUR GARDEN

The hooting call of the owl is surely one of the most familiar sounds of the countryside, yet the bird itself is rarely seen, due to its predominantly nocturnal lifestyle. Occasionally, an owl may be discovered at a daytime roost, where it can allow a very close approach.

Nestboxes come in all sorts of shapes and sizes, each designed to attract a particular species, or group of species. As hole nesters, owls can be enticed to use nestboxes with this specially-designed "chimney box". Made to resemble a hollowed-out piece of wood, it should be attached firmly to the underside of a sturdy branch, using wire or straps.

Owls are highly sedentary, spending most of their lives in a very small area, even during the harsh winter weather. They are most often found in gardens near mixed or deciduous woodland, or those with plenty of mature trees in which the owls can breed and roost and where they hunt their rodent prey.

Owls are early nesters, so make sure you put the box up in autumn or early winter. Ideally you should check to make sure there are owls in the local area first, which will maximize your chances of success. Owls lay between two and five eggs, which they incubate for four weeks. The young often leave the nest before they are fully fledged.

Step 1: Setting out the slabs

Step 2: Cutting the wood

Step 3: Using the gouge

Step 4: Dry-run put-together

Step 5: Drilling the nail holes

Step 6: Putting together

CONSTRUCTION DETAILS FOR THE OWL CHIMNEY BOX

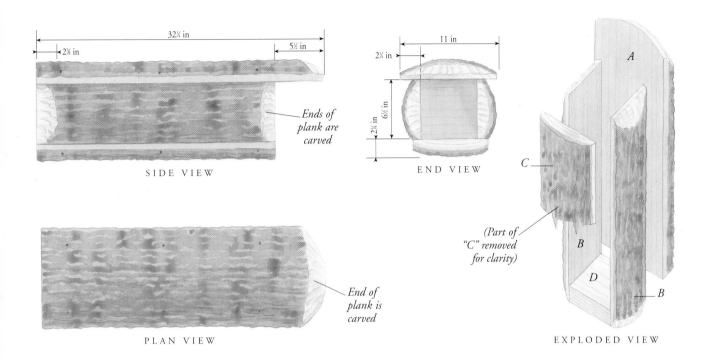

32¼ in

2⅝ in

5½ in

Ends of plank are carved

SIDE VIEW

11 in

2¼ in

6½ in

2¼ in

END VIEW

A

C

(Part of "C" removed for clarity)

B

D

B

End of plank is carved

PLAN VIEW

EXPLODED VIEW

HOW TO MAKE THE PROJECT

Step 1: Setting out the slabs Check your chosen wood for potential problems such as dead knots, splits and spongy areas, and avoid them. Use the pencil, ruler, straight-edge and square to set out all the measurements on the sawn face of the wood.

Step 2: Cutting the wood Clamp the wood firmly in the vice, bridging it across the open vice, with the bar clamp clamping down the tail end of the slab. Wipe a small amount of vegetable oil over the blade of the hand saw – to keep the blade moving freely and to stop it rusting – and cut out the pieces. Use the bow saw to cut the leading end of the roof slab (A) to a rounded finish.

Step 3: Using the gouge Butt the end of the workpiece hard up against a bench stop (a piece of plywood nailed to the bench) and use the mallet and gouge to cut the end of the wood to a gently sloped finish. Do this on the leading end of the roof slab (A), and on both ends of the side slabs (B). Leave the gouge marks showing.

Step 4: Dry-run put-together Support the base slab (C) in the vice and establish the position of the two side slabs (B) and the end piece (D). Mark out registration lines so that you know precisely how the wood comes together.

Step 5: Drilling the nail holes With the drill bit, drill holes for the nails to prevent the wood from splitting. Do this on the base slab (C) and the roof slab (A).

Step 6: Putting together Use the claw hammer to nail the base slab (C) to both side slabs (B) and the end piece (D), then turn the whole work over and nail the roof slab in place. The nails must not protrude inside the box.

MOUNTING

Find a good-size branch (one that is angled upwards from the trunk) at a point about 16 feet up the tree. Position the box with its entrance out of direct sunlight and with some shelter from the elements, and then secure it with three or more straps of galvanized wire.

JAPANESE BIRD BATH

his project draws its inspiration from the wonderful, calming imagery of traditional Japanese Zen gardens. The monolithic block of wood mounted on the tree stump takes on much the same role as the Japanese sentinel or guardian stone, the carved ripples on the surface of the wood symbolize waves, and the attractive hollow filled with water makes a perfect bird bath – all beautiful!

DESIGN NOTES

While in many ways this is the simplest of projects – not much more than a slab of wood with a carved hollow – the actual size and weight of the wood does make for difficulties. On the other hand, the wood is so heavy that it doesn't need to be held or clamped. We found that the best way of working was simply to set the slab on the ground (under cover), and then to move around it. As for the choice of wood, it is vital to pick an easy-to-carve hardwood. We chose a slab of straight-grained, knot-free basswood. When you are selecting the slab of wood, make sure that it is well seasoned – meaning that the wood has been allowed to dry for at least a year. American basswood is particularly suited to this project as it is relatively easy to acquire and simple to carve – it is generally a wood that can't be bettered. This is an especially good project for those new to woodcarving.

Materials
- American basswood slab, 30 in long, 5⅞ in thick and 23⅛ in wide (A)
- Tree section, about 18⅛ in long and 16 in in diameter (B)

Tools
- Pencil, ruler, straight-edge and felt-tip marker
- Tracing paper, 30 in long and 23⅛ in wide

- Electric drill
- Forstner drill bits, 1 in and 2 in
- Adze
- Wooden mallets, heavyweight and lightweight
- Straight gouges, 1 in and 1½ in
- Bent gouge, 1 in
- V-section tool

BATH TIME FOR BIRDS

A well-made bird bath is one of the essential ingredients in creating a truly bird-friendly garden, giving the birds a regular source of clean water to drink and bathe in. This design is practical and sturdy, as well as being a very attractive piece of garden furniture.

Birds come in all shapes and sizes, so a bird bath needs to have a "shallow end" and a "deep end". Keep the bath filled on a daily basis, perhaps more frequently in hot weather. Every week or so, give your bird bath a thorough clean (you can use household cleaners, but rinse the bath thoroughly afterwards to remove any trace of chemicals). In harsh winter weather, make sure the water doesn't freeze by topping it up with warm water from time to time.

Most birds bathe at least once a day, generally in the morning or evening. Bathing is vital for birds to keep their plumage clean and their feathers in tip-top condition. It is especially important in winter, as it allows them to fluff out their feathers properly to insulate themselves against the cold. As natural sources of water such as lakes and ponds may be some distance away, many garden birds depend on those provided by us, either in the form of bird baths or garden ponds.

Ideally your bird bath should be sited in an open area, to minimize the chances of cats sneaking up on the birds as they wash or drink.

Step 1: Setting out the design

Step 2: Drilling out the waste

Step 3: Roughing out with the adze and gouge

Step 4: Hollowing out

Step 5: Cutting the V-grooves

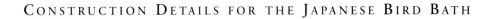

CONSTRUCTION DETAILS FOR THE JAPANESE BIRD BATH

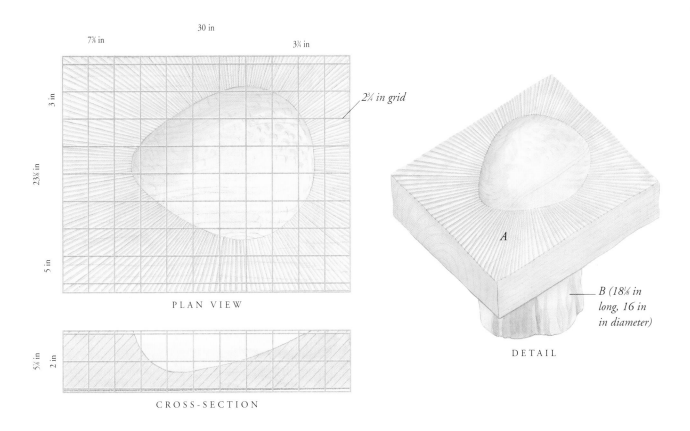

30 in

7⅞ in

3¼ in

3 in

23⅛ in

5 in

2¾ in grid

A

PLAN VIEW

B (18⅛ in
long, 16 in
in diameter)

DETAIL

5⅜ in

2 in

CROSS-SECTION

HOW TO MAKE THE PROJECT

Step 1: Setting out the design Trace out the design at full size. With a pencil, press-transfer the traced lines through to the face of the wood (A). Establish the center of the hollow and use the straight-edge and felt-tip marker to rule lines that radiate out from the center.

Step 2: Drilling out the waste Remember that the hollow needs to be deepest at the narrow end. Use the drill to clear the bulk of the waste. Start with the larger forstner bit for boring out the widest and deepest holes, and then follow up with the smaller bit.

Step 3: Roughing out with the adze and gouge Use the adze to cut down to the depth of the drilled holes. Hold the adze at a fairly flat angle, and work from the drawn line through to the center. Be careful not to sink the blade too deeply. With the mallets and the 1½ inch straight gouge, tidy up the deepest part of the hollow.

Step 4: Hollowing out Use the 1 inch straight gouge to establish the edge of the hollow – you need a nice, clean smooth curve – and skim the surface to a smooth finish with the bent gouge. Work with smaller and smaller strokes until you achieve a fine, ripple-textured finish.

Step 5: Cutting the V-grooves Hold the V-section tool at a low angle and work from the edge of the hollow towards the edge of the wood. Be very careful not to dig too deeply into the wood. Continue until the pattern of grooves completely covers the surface of the wood.

MOUNTING

When you have selected a suitable site – preferably within view of your house and well away from prowling cats and noisy children – set the tree stump (B) in place, check that it is firm and level, and then get help to lift the slab into position.

BRAIN-TEASER FEEDER

T*he whole idea of the brain-teaser feeder is that it allows small birds to comfortably eat their fill, while preventing big birds or pests such as squirrels from getting in. The small birds can just about squeeze between the wooden dowels, and then on through the wire mesh to the peanuts that are contained in the mesh core.*

DESIGN NOTES

The brain-teaser feeder is made up of seven primary elements. There is a large green disc roof that doubles as a lid, two smaller yellow discs and a ring of wooden dowels that form the outer cage or first barrier, an inner wall of wire mesh that forms the second barrier, and a central mesh cage to hold the nuts. The whole work is held together with a twist of galvanized wire.

To fill the central cage with nuts, you simply slide the green disc up the wire, and trickle the nuts through the hole at the center of the topmost yellow disc. If you like working with a compass, and are adept with a scroll saw, this project will keep you absorbed. When you mount the project in the garden, you have to bear in mind that while the feeder must be within reach, it also needs to be away from predators.

Materials

- Exterior plywood, disc 12 in in diameter and ¼ in thick (A)
- Exterior plywood, 2 x discs 7⅞ in in diameter and ⅜ in thick (B) (C)
- Doweling, 12 x lengths of 7⅞ in, ⅜ in in diameter (D)
- Exterior plywood, disc 2⅜ in in diameter and ⅜ in thick (E)
- Exterior plywood, disc 3⅜ in in diameter and ⅜ in thick (F)
- Exterior plywood, disc 1½ in in diameter and ⅜ in thick (G)
- Wire mesh, 13¾ in long, 6¼ in wide and 1 x 1 in grid (H)
- Wire mesh, 7⅛ in long, 6¼ in wide, ¼ x ¼ in grid (I)
- Exterior-grade PVA wood glue
- Panel nails, ½ in and 1 in
- Acrylic paint, green and yellow
- Matte exterior-quality varnish
- Galvanized wire, 4 x lengths of 21⅛ in (J)

Tools

- Workbench with vice
- Pencil, ruler, square and compass
- Scroll saw
- Electric drill
- Bench drill press
- Forstner drill bits, ¹⁄₁₆ in, ⅜ in and 1½ in
- Long-nose pliers, wire snips
- Pin hammer
- Sandpaper and sanding block
- Paintbrush, ¾ in

BAN UNWELCOME GUESTS

T*here's nothing more annoying than putting out expensive, high-quality food for the birds, only to watch it being eaten by squirrels – especially if they destroy the feeder in the process. So why not try making a feeder which lets the birds in – while keeping the squirrels out?*

The design is simple but effective: thin dowel rods allow small birds such as sparrows, finches and even – at a squeeze – starlings, to reach the food. As a bonus, this feeder also acts as a partial deterrent to cats, which find it hard to reach the feeding birds.

The only potential drawback is that some birds, particularly shyer species, may be wary of entering the bars at first. However, once they get used to it you should find that the birds soon take advantage of a squirrel-proof food supply – and you save money! The only losers are the squirrels, who hopefully will head off for easier pickings in a neighbor's garden.

Step 1: Setting out the discs

Step 2: Sawing the discs

Step 3: Drilling the dowel holes

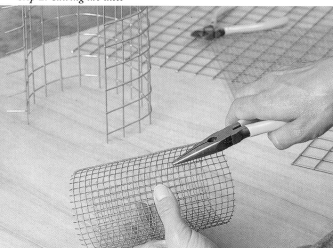

Step 4: Cutting and shaping the wire mesh

Step 5: Gluing and painting

Step 6: Fitting together

CONSTRUCTION DETAILS FOR THE BRAIN-TEASER FEEDER

12 in diameter, ¼ in thick

3⅛ in

7⅞ in

6¼ in

1⅜ in

7⅞ in diameter, ⅜ in thick

⅜ in dowel, 7⅞ in long

FRONT VIEW

7⅞ in diameter, ⅜ in thick

PLAN VIEW

UNDERSIDE DETAIL

G (under A)

A

B

F (with 2⁵⁄₁₆ in diameter hole sawn into it)

I

D

H

hole for wire

hole for dowel

E

C

J

EXPLODED VIEW

HOW TO MAKE THE PROJECT

Step 1: Setting out the discs Use the compass to set out the green lid (A), the plug (G), the two yellow discs (B and C), the peanut cage bottom disk (E), and the disc-ring (F) for over the top of the peanut cage.

Step 2: Sawing the discs Having drawn out the six discs, carefully cut them out with the scroll saw. Work at a steady pace in order to achieve clean, smooth curves.

Step 3: Drilling the dowel holes Sandwich the two 7⅞ inch discs (B and C), set out the position of the 12 dowel holes and, using the drill press, drill them with the ⅜ inch forstner bit. Separate the discs and then use the 1½ inch bit to run a hole through one of the discs.

Step 4: Cutting and shaping the wire mesh To make the outer cage (H) and the peanut cage (I), cut the wire mesh to size with the wire snips. Leave extra "fingers" of wire on one mating edge. Bend the mesh into shape and fold the fingers around the other edge with the pliers.

Step 5: Gluing and painting Glue the three small discs (E, F and G) in place and fix with ½ inch nails. Drill ⅜ inch holes through the centers of the lid and base. Smooth all surfaces with sandpaper. Apply a coat of acrylic paint. When dry, coat them with matte varnish. Make up the central rod (J) from a twist of four wires.

Step 6: Fitting together Slide the dowels (D) in place and fix with the 1 inch panel nails. Drill a ring of holes for the outer cage with the ¹⁄₁₆ inch drill bit. Sit the "fingers" of the cage in the holes. Locate the peanut cage in the holding ring and slide it into position. Fit the green lid, slide the twisted central holding rod through the whole work, and loop the ends to secure it.

MOUNTING

Select a sheltered site, such as under a tree or house eaves, and position the feeder at a height that is comfortable to reach. Hang it up with wire or strong twine. Finally, fill the inner cage with nuts, and wait for your first visitors.

RUSTIC BIRD FEEDER

Thi*s project has been fired by childhood memories. When I was about eight, I dreamed of being an outdoors man like Davy Crockett. Armed only with a penknife, I used to roam through the woods making bows and arrows and fishing rods. The Rustic Bird Feeder has been inspired by these memories.* (ALAN)

DESIGN NOTES

This design uses green ash, oak, and pine pieces which can be found in nature or at a lumber yard. All the diameter measurements are a very general guide. You will have to purchase or find the nearest available size, and then whittle and trim back to the given dimensions. Part of the joy of working with green wood is that every single stick and pole is unique.

FEEDING HABITS

From a bird's point of view, the bird table is the centerpiece of your garden. It enables you to provide a wide variety of different foods, suitable for many different kinds of birds which feed at different levels. Perching birds such as sparrows and starlings will feed on the solid base, while you can hang extra feeders for tits and finches. Meanwhile, ground-feeding birds such as pigeons, doves, thrushes and blackbirds will feed on spilled food beneath the table.

On a cautionary note, a poorly placed bird table may enable cats or sparrow hawks to help themselves to an easy meal by snatching one of the feeding birds. It is best to set your table a little away from nearby trees, bushes or fence posts, though not so far that the birds can't use them as cover to approach.

Always keep your bird table well stocked, and make sure you clear up any uneaten food every couple of days, as well as giving the new table a good scrub with soap and water every month or so.

Materials

- 4 x ash poles, 69 in long and $1\frac{1}{4}$ – $1\frac{1}{2}$ inches in diameter (A)
- 4 x ash poles, $25\frac{1}{2}$ in long and $1\frac{1}{4}$ – $1\frac{1}{2}$ inches in diameter (B)
- 4 x ash poles, $16\frac{3}{4}$ in long and $1\frac{1}{4}$ – $1\frac{1}{2}$ inches in diameter (C)
- Rough-sawn oak board, $18\frac{3}{4}$ in long, 1 in thick and 16 in wide (D)
- 2 x sawn oak rods, $18\frac{3}{4}$ in long, $\frac{3}{4}$ in thick and $\frac{3}{4}$ in wide (E)
- 2 x sawn oak rods, 14 in long, $\frac{3}{4}$ in thick and $\frac{3}{4}$ in wide (F)
- Ash stick, $23\frac{3}{8}$ in long, 1 – $1\frac{1}{4}$ inches in diameter (G)
- 2 x sawn oak boards, $16\frac{3}{4}$ in long, $\frac{3}{4}$ in thick and $10\frac{13}{16}$ in wide (H)
- 6 x sawn pine slats, $17\frac{1}{8}$ in long, $\frac{5}{16}$ in thick and $5\frac{7}{8}$ in wide (I)
- 4 x cut pegs, $5\frac{7}{8}$ in long and 1 inch in diameter (J)
- 4 x cut pegs, 5 in long and 1 inch in diameter (K)
- 2 x sawn oak boards, $17\frac{1}{8}$ in long, $\frac{3}{4}$ in thick and $9\frac{7}{8}$ in wide (L)
- 4 x cut pegs, $6\frac{1}{4}$ in long, 1 inch in diameter (M)
- 2 x sawn oak rods, $17\frac{1}{8}$ in long, $\frac{3}{4}$ in thick and $\frac{3}{4}$ in wide (N)
- 4 x cut pegs, $4\frac{3}{4}$ in long, 1 inch in diameter (O)
- Panel pins, 1 in and $1\frac{1}{2}$ in
- Strong twine

Tools

- Workbench with vice and bar clamp
- Pencil, ruler, square and compass
- Sash clamp
- Drawknife
- Penknife
- Brace
- Auger bits, $\frac{3}{8}$ in and $1\frac{3}{16}$ in
- Hand saw
- Pin hammer

Step 1: Using the drawknife

Step 2: Boring out the peg holes

Step 3: Nailing the roof boards

Step 4: Making the food table

Step 5: Attaching the roof in place

Step 6: Finishing

CONSTRUCTION DETAILS FOR THE RUSTIC BIRD FEEDER

FRONT
VIEW

17⅛ in

I

G

18¾ in

J

E

D

B

25½ in long,
1¼ – 1½ in
diameter

C

A

K

16¼ in long,
1¼ – 1½ in diameter

SIDE VIEW

FRONT VIEW DETAIL

16¾ in

16 in

N

2 in

L

9⅝ in

H

2 in

F

M

O

69 in long,
1¼ – 1½ in diameter

SIDE VIEW DETAIL

HOW TO MAKE THE PROJECT

Step 1: Using the drawknife Use the pencil, square and compass to set out the components. Put the poles in the vice and bridge them across the sash clamp. Hold the drawknife with the bevel on the underside (to control the depth of the cut) and trim the poles to size. Rerun this procedure for all the large round sections. Use the penknife to whittle all the pegs to shape.

Step 2: Boring out the peg holes Use the brace and the appropriate auger bit to bore out the holes – ⅜ in for the pegs, and 1³⁄₁₆ in for the two roof-board holes. Use the bench bar clamp to secure the difficult-to-hold shapes.

Step 3: Nailing the roof boards Cut the roof triangles (H) to shape with the hand saw and nail the roof boards and slats (I) in place. Overlap the slats by 1½ in and nail the top slats to the oak rods (N). Use as many of the 1 in and 1½ in panel nails as necessary.

Step 4: Making the food table Use the 1½ in panel nails to nail the ¾ in-square rods (E and F) around the top edge of the sawn oak board (D) to make a ¾ in-deep tray. Drive the panel nails in from both sides – down through the rods, and up through the board.

Step 5: Attaching the roof Attach the basic frame of the structure together with the wooden pegs and push the ridge stick (G) into position through the roof.

Step 6: Finishing Slide the tray in place – so that the pegs (M) slot down between the supporting horizontal cross-poles (B). Finally, lash the joints with strong twine.

MOUNTING

Select a site in view of the house, make sure that the main poles are well spread and secure, put some food scraps on the tray, and then sit back and enjoy the action.

FEEDING STATION

The feeding station is reminiscent of Pennsylvanian German barns – lots of arched windows, steep roofs and color. With bunkers jam-packed full of peanuts, and with a bar for hanging lumps of lard and the like, it is a paradise for birds.

DESIGN NOTES

The clever thing about this design is that in bad weather, the birds can go inside and feed in comfort.

The scroll-sawing procedure has been simplified, with the dimensions sized so that the sawing can be achieved without the need to drill pilot holes. All you do is saw from the bottom edge straight up the door-window center-line, cutting away the waste in two halves.

Materials

- 2 x pieces exterior plywood, 18¾ in long, ⅜ in thick and 19⅛ in wide (A)
- 2 x pieces exterior plywood, 13¾ in long, ³⁄₁₆ in thick and 4⅜ in wide (B)
- 2 x pieces exterior plywood, 13¾ in long, ³⁄₁₆ in thick and 5½ in wide (C)
- 2 x pieces exterior plywood, 13¾ in long, ³⁄₁₆ in thick and 5¼ in wide (D)
- 2 x pieces exterior plywood, 12¼ in long, ⅜ in thick and 4 in wide (E)
- 2 x pieces exterior plywood, 12¼ in long, ⅜ in thick and 3¼ in wide (F)
- 2 x pieces exterior plywood, 12¼ in long, ⅜ in thick and 3¼ in wide (G)
- Exterior plywood, 27⅞ in long, ⅜ in thick and 23⅜ in wide (H)
- Pine, 55¾ in long, ¾ x ¾ in square section (I)
- Pine, 47½ in long, ¾ x ¾ in square section (J)
- Exterior plywood, 12¼ in long, ⅜ in thick and 18⅜ in wide (K)
- Exterior plywood, 12¼ in long, ⅜ in thick and 11¾ in wide (L)
- Exterior plywood 27⅞ in long, ³⁄₁₆ in thick and ⅞ in wide (M)
- Doweling, 19⅜ in long, ⅜ inch in diameter (N)
- Wire mesh, 19⅜ in long, 19⅜ in wide (this allows for cutting waste), ¼ x ¼ in grid (O)
- 2 x rustic fence posts, 6½ ft long and 2¾ inches in diameter (P)
- 6 x steel flap hinges, 1½ in long and 1¼ in wide
- Steel countersunk screws to fit the hinges, ³⁄₁₆ in
- Nails, 3¼ in
- Panel nails, ½ in and ¾ in
- Staples, ³⁄₁₆ in
- Exterior-grade PVA wood glue
- Acrylic paint, brick red and blue
- Clear exterior-quality varnish

Tools

- Workbench with vice
- Pencil, ruler, engineer's square and compass
- Scroll saw
- Electric drill
- Bench drill press
- Forstner drill bit, 1½ in
- Screwdriver
- Long-nose pliers
- Pin and claw hammers
- Paintbrush, 1 in
- Sandpaper and sanding block

BIRD NOTES

If you want to provide a real gourmet service for your garden birds, why not make a full-scale feeding station. This is a high-class bird table, with different areas for different kinds of food, including seeds, fruit and scraps.

As with bird tables, it is essential that you put your feeding station in the right place. Keep it well-stocked, clear away spilt or uneaten food, and clean it regularly.

Keep a log of which birds use it, how often, and for how long. Also, watch out for unusual visitors, especially in winter, when harsh weather often forces birds from the surrounding countryside to venture into gardens in search of food. Look out for titmice, nuthatches, woodpeckers and winter thrushes.

Step 1: Setting out the plywood

Step 2: Scroll-sawing the door-windows

Step 3: Nailing the walls together

Step 4: Painting and fitting

Step 5: Attaching the wire mesh

Step 6: Attaching the roof

CONSTRUCTION DETAILS FOR THE FEEDING STATION

13¾ in
12¼ in
3 in | 3 in | 3 in
1½ in
⅜ in

*2 in
1½ in hole

*1½ in

*1½ in

B
E
C
F
D
G

M

⁵⁄₁₆ in thick

¾ x ¾ in section

23⅝ in

SIDE VIEW

*Position of center-line from bottom edge of component

4⅝ in
4 in
2⅜ in
2⅜ in
2 in
1½ in
18⅜ in
2⅜ in
¾ in
3¼ in

3⅜ in

1³⁄₁₆ in radius

1¹⁄₁₆ in

1½ in hole
⅜ in thick

O
A
P
N

27⅞ in

FRONT VIEW

(hinges fitted 1½ in from outside edge)

J
L
K
I
H

Drainage hole

EXPLODED VIEW

HOW TO MAKE THE PROJECT

Step 1: Setting out the plywood Use the pencil, ruler, square and compass to set out the design on the plywood. Make the gable ends (A) identical and draw center-lines up through the door-windows.

Step 2: Scroll-sawing the door-windows Run the saw cut straight in from the bottom edge of the wood and up the center-line. Maneuver the wood so as to work to the waste side of the drawn line, and exit along the same cut.

Step 3: Nailing the walls together With the bench drill press and appropriate forstner bit, bore out the various round windows. Glue the walls (A, E, F and G) together and attach with the ¾ inch panel nails. Screw the inside floors (L and K) in place, ensuring everything is square.

Step 4: Painting and fitting Paint the whole work inside and out. Use sandpaper to rub down the paint and achieve an aged effect. Paint with varnish.

Step 5: Attaching the wire mesh Use the staples to hold the wire mesh (O) in place. When you come to the top bunker, bend the wire mesh round in a continuous curve – so that the single piece forms the bottom of the bunker as well as covering the round window holes. Hold the staples with the long-nose pliers and hammer them in.

Step 6: Attaching the roof Glue and nail one of the top roof flaps (B) (the other is hinged), glue and nail the middle flaps (C) and attach the bottom flaps with hinges. Use glue and nails to make the platform (H, I and J).

MOUNTING

Bang one of the posts (P) into the ground, and attach the platform to the top with the 3¼ inch nails and the claw hammer. Screw the feeder house to the platform. Cut the other post into four equal lengths and nail these in place under the platform, making a bracketed structure. Nail the dowel rod (N) to the main post.

CARVED DECOY DUCK RAFT FEEDER

*T*raditionally, the whole idea of the carved decoy duck is that you stake it out at the side of a lake, wait for real ducks to be attracted, jump up with your gun, and... bang, you have food for the pot! With this project, you simply forget the "bang", and enjoy the delightful sight of ducks feeding around the decoy and its raft.

DESIGN NOTES

Duck carving is easier than it looks. You must choose a straight-grained wood that is easy to carve. American basswood works well, or even some species of straight-grained pine – as long as the wood cuts easily and comes from a sustainable source. We favor using a bandsaw for cutting out the blank, a flat chisel for cutting the mortise, and a straight gouge and a knife for the modelling.

Materials

- Basswood, 12⅜ in long, 4 in thick and 5⅞ in wide (A)
- Basswood, 5⅜ in long, 1½ in thick and 4¼ in wide (B)
- 2 x pine posts, 26 in long and 2⅜ in in diameter (C)
- 2 x pine boards, 23⅜ in long, 1 in thick and 9 in wide (D)
- Exterior-grade PVA wood glue
- Nails, 2⁵⁄₁₆ in
- Water-based drawing inks, yellow, viridian, vermilion, peat brown and black
- Tracing paper
- Exterior-quality matte varnish

Tools

- Workbench with vice and bar clamp
- Pencil, ruler, square and compass
- Scroll saw
- Paring chisel, 1³⁄₁₆ in
- Sash clamp
- Carving mallets, heavyweight and lightweight
- Straight gouge, 1 in wide
- Knife
- Sandpaper and sanding block
- Artist's watercolor brushes, fine, medium and large
- Paintbrush, 1 in
- Claw hammer

DUCK TRAP

*T*he original "decoy" was a large device made from wood and netting, used by hunters to trap wild ducks. However, the word can also refer to model ducks placed in the decoy to lure down wild birds, trapping them for food or to lay eggs.

The practice was originally Dutch – indeed the word "decoy" is derived from a Dutch word meaning "duck trap". The use of decoys soon spread throughout northern Europe, and was especially popular during the sixteenth and seventeenth centuries. The practice gradually died out, and today the few remaining decoys are used for scientific research.

Today, wooden decoy ducks can be used either to attract wild ducks to a garden pond, or simply to provide an attractive decorative feature in the garden. They can be left natural, or painted to resemble wild duck species.

The duck on our raft feeder is based on the Mallard. The male Mallard is one of the most handsome and distinctive of ducks, with a bottle-green head and dark magenta breast. Mallards are usually found in freshwater habitats such as lakes, but may visit small garden ponds, or even graze on a damp lawn.

Other waterbirds, such as gallinule, are regular visitors to gardens near lakes or ponds, especially during winter weather, when usual sources of water are iced over.

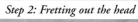

Step 1: Setting out the wood

Step 2: Fretting out the head

Step 3: Cutting the mortise

Step 4: Roughing out

Step 5: Carving the form

Step 6: Modelling and sanding

Step 7: Painting and finishing

CONSTRUCTION DETAILS FOR THE CARVED DECOY DUCK RAFT FEEDER

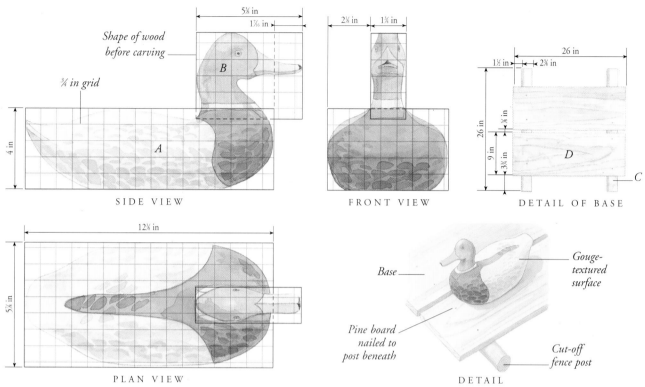

SIDE VIEW

FRONT VIEW

DETAIL OF BASE

PLAN VIEW

DETAIL

HOW TO MAKE THE PROJECT

Step 1: Setting out the wood Use the ruler and compass to set out the body slab (A) – 12⅜ in long, with a 2¼ in radius at each end. Trace the head image (use the grid for guidance) on to the 1½ in-thick slab (B).

Step 2: Fretting out the head Fret out the head profile on the scroll saw. Work at a steady pace, with the line of cut always slightly to the waste side of the drawn line.

Step 3: Cutting the mortise Draw out the mortise at 3⅜ in long, ⅝ in deep and 1½ in wide. Use the paring chisel to cut it out.

Step 4: Roughing out Secure the workpiece with the bar clamp and the sash clamp, and use the heavyweight mallet and gouge to round over all the sawn corners.

Step 5: Carving the form Use the lightweight mallet and gouge to carve the form as shown in the front, side and plan views. Only cut in the direction of the grain.

Step 6: Modelling and sanding When you have achieved a good form – with the surface nicely dappled with gouge and knife cuts – use the sandpaper to sand down the duck to a smooth finish.

Step 7: Painting and finishing Use the watercolor brushes to lay on thin coats of color: yellow for the bill, viridian for the head, a mix of vermilion and peat brown for the breast, and black for the eyes. When it is dry, use sandpaper to rub through the ink to reveal the underlying wood. Brush on a coat of matte varnish. Finally, set the two 26 in posts (C) about 16 in apart and nail the boards (D) in place with the claw hammer. If the nail points protrude, hammer them over.

MOUNTING
Choose a sheltered position at the water's edge, and set the raft and the duck in place. If you are worried about losing the duck you could screw it to the raft and fix the whole work with stakes.

FOLK ART FEEDER HOUSE

*T*his unusual and decorative bird house/feeder table has been inspired by American folk art of the eighteenth and nineteenth centuries. The gabled roof, wide balconies, arched doorways, heavy shutters, hooped balustrade and distressed paint finish make it slightly kitsch, with just a dash of New Orleans.

DESIGN NOTES

While this house may be viewed as "over the top" – it is perhaps overly large, too colorful, and just a tad too decorative – it is for all that a very successful design. The bright, eye-catching colors seem to attract the birds, the house provides shelter, and the hooped balustrade prevents the food from rolling off the balconies. From the human perspective, the whole house is simply good fun, and much favored by children and adults alike. If you enjoy challenging woodwork, like decoration, and want a large splash of color in the garden, then this is a project you can revel in. While at first sight the design looks somewhat difficult – all those bits and pieces coming together at different angles – it is in fact quite simple to make.

Materials

- Exterior plywood, 23⅝ in long, ⅜ in thick and 23⅝ in wide (A)
- Exterior plywood, 19⅝ in long, ⅜ in thick and 19⅝ in wide (B)
- 4 x pieces of exterior plywood, 22 in long, ⅜ in thick and 13⅞ in wide (C)
- 4 x pieces of exterior plywood, 16⅞ in long, ³⁄₁₆ in thick and 11½ in wide (D)
- 4 x wooden balls, about 1½ in in diameter (E)
- ³⁄₁₆ in threaded rod, 11¹³⁄₁₆ in long, with two nuts and two washers (F)
- Rattan, 55¾ ft length (G)
- Plastic lid, about 3¼ in in diameter
- Exterior-grade PVA wood glue
- Panel nails, ½ in
- Acrylic paint, white, brick red, mid-green and ochre
- Artist's oil paint, burnt umber
- Exterior-quality matte varnish
- Wire or rope to hang

Tools

- Workbench with vice
- Pencil, ruler and compass
- Engineer's square
- Hand saw
- Scroll saw with fine blade
- Pin hammer
- Paintbrush, 1 in
- Sandpaper and sanding block
- Electric drill
- General purpose drill bit, ⅛ in
- Long-nose pliers and wire snips

PEANUT FEEDERS

A peanut feeder will attract a wide variety of birds to your garden. The rigid wire mesh design allows birds to take a firm grip, so they can peck off morsels of peanut (small birds could choke on whole nuts). Hang it from the base of your feeder house or bird table, or if you prefer, from a post or tree in a suitable position.

Peanut feeders are suitable for a wide range of species, especially chickadees, sparrows and finches such as the Siskin. Good-quality peanuts are packed full of energy, allowing the birds to make the most of the limited time available for feeding during the short winter days, and increasing their chances of survival.

During harsh winter weather, you may need to replenish the feeder several times a day, though when natural food is plentiful it can last several weeks. Try experimenting with different colored feeders: although most human beings like subtle colors such as green, it seems that birds prefer bright blue, red or silver!

CONSTRUCTION DETAILS FOR THE FOLK ART FEEDER HOUSE

13⅞ in

3¾ in   3¼ in   1½ in

6¼ in   6¼ in

4⅞ in

22 in

4⅞ in

3¾ in

4 in

1½ in radius

1½ in radius

Roof is first painted green, then red, and finally sanded to reveal the underlying color

G

These shutters are the waste from cutting out the windows

FRONT VIEW

23⅜ in
19⅜ in
16¾ in

23⅜ in
19⅜ in
16¾ in

PLAN VIEW

Rattan arch skips over two holes

Rattan is a tight fit in the holes

Holes, ⅛ in deep, set at ⅜ in intervals

HOOPED BALUSTRADE DETAIL

68

F (threaded rod bent
into a hook shape)

H (found plastic lid)

Balls cut to
fit the shape
of the roof

Scrap of plywood
inside the roof

Roof cut and
notched to fit
over gable wall

E

Roof panels are
glued and nailed
to the walls

D

Strip of waste
plywood used to
support floor panel

D

Balcony fits
tightly over
walls and is
nailed from
the inside

C

B

B

Strip of waste
plywood used for
balustrade rail

A

Window shutters
are nailed and
glued to walls

Blocks of waste
plywood glued
and screwed to
the floor

EXPLODED VIEW

Step 1: Setting out the design

Step 2: Fretting out the design

Step 3: Nailing the walls

Step 4: Fitting the roof

Step 5: Attaching the floor and first coat of paint

Step 6: Sanding and texturing

Step 7: Fitting the balustrade rail arches and ridge balls

Step 8: Finishing

HOW TO MAKE THE PROJECT

Step 1: Setting out the design Study the design and consider how the components best fit the plywood – to minimize waste. Use the pencil, compass, engineer's square and ruler to set out the various parts.

Step 2: Fretting out the design Use the hand saw and the scroll saw to cut out the pieces. In the knowledge that the door-window waste becomes the shutters, run the line of cut straight up the door-window center-line, from the bottom of the wall up to the head of the top window.

Step 3: Nailing the walls Mitre the corners of the walls (C) on the scroll saw. Smear glue on the 45° faces, join, and attach with the panel nails.

Step 4: Fitting the roof Fit the two long roof boards (D), and cut the other two roof boards (D) to fit. Glue and nail the roof panels to the walls.

Step 5: Attaching the floor and first coat of paint Cut the floors (A and B) to size and attach them in place with the ½ inch panel nails. Construct the raised balustrade strips from offcuts, and glue and nail them in place around the edge of the balustrade and the main floor. Paint everything white, and when dry, add further coats of paint as follows. Roof: green, outer walls: red, floors: green, balustrades: green, shutters and decorations: ochre.

Step 6: Sanding and texturing When the paint is dry, use the sandpaper to carefully rub away areas of paint to expose the white underneath. Paint on a third coat of paint – roof: red, outer walls: green, floors: red, balustrades: red, shutters and decorations: ochre – and repeat the sanding procedure. Glue the shutters and discs in place. Mix a little artist's oil paint into the varnish. Paint all the surfaces, inside and out, with varnish.

Step 7: Fitting the balustrade rail arches and ridge balls Drill ⅛ inch holes at ⅜ inch intervals along the top of the balustrade strips. Use wire snips to cut the rattan (G) into 4 inch lengths, and the long-nose pliers to push it into the holes with the arches overlapping (each arch skips two holes). Glue the balls (E) in place on the ridge, and give them a coat of the burnt umber varnish.

Step 8: Finishing With the pliers, bend the threaded rod into a hook shape (F) and run it down through the plastic lid (H) and the roof. Spread the load by having a piece of scrap plywood on the inside. Attach with the washers and nuts.

MOUNTING

Select a suitable site, such as a stout branch or a garden structure. Use wire or rope to hang the house about 6½ feet from the ground.

EDWARDIAN-STYLE DOVECOTE

Nothing evokes the English cottage garden quite so well as a dovecote. Painted white and mounted high up on a gable, the cote provides a safe haven not only for doves but for all manner of birds. Just imagine a warm summer's evening, the sun low in the sky, with doves slowly circling, about to come to roost – wonderful!

DESIGN NOTES

This design looks quite complicated – lots of fancy brackets, arched doors, landing platforms, all topped off with a roof finial – but it is in fact a relatively straightforward project. The forms are cut out with a hand-held portable jigsaw and a bench scroll saw, waste pieces are cleverly used as trim, most of it is made from ⅜ inch exterior plywood, and the making stages are surprisingly easy. There is no complicated chisel work or joint cutting and the whole project is put together with screws.

LOVE DOVES

Birds have been kept and bred in captivity since time immemorial. One of the most popular groups of birds amongst aviculturists is that of pigeons and doves. They are attractive, easily tamed, and breed throughout the year, enabling many varieties to be produced by artificial selection, such as the exotic-looking Fantail Pigeon.

Descendants of the wild Rock Dove also have excellent homing abilities, enabling them to be used for racing, or for carrying messages. During the Second World War, many allied servicemen owed their lives to messages delivered by carrier pigeons.

Pigeons and doves are kept in lofts, or dovecotes, of which this is an ornamental version designed as an attractive item of garden furniture. It is unlikely that wild birds would use the dovecote, although you might try putting out seed on the ledges to attract the White-crowned Pigeon found in the eastern United States.

Materials

- 2 x pieces exterior plywood, 35½ in long, ⅜ in thick and 23⅜ in wide (A) (B)
- 2 x pieces exterior plywood, 31½ in long, ⅜ in thick and 11¹³⁄₁₆ in wide (C)
- 3 x pieces exterior plywood, 23 in long, ⅜ in thick and 11¹³⁄₁₆ in wide (D)(E)(F)
- Exterior plywood, 22⁷⁄₁₆ in long, ⅜ in thick and 7⅜ in wide (G)
- Exterior plywood, 22⁷⁄₁₆ in long, ⅜ in thick and 9⁹⁄₁₆ in wide (H)
- 2 x pieces exterior plywood, 7¾ in long, ⅜ in thick and 6½ in wide (I)
- 4 x pieces exterior plywood, 5⅜ in long, ⅜ in thick and 4⅛ in wide (J)
- 2 x pieces exterior plywood, 9½ in long, ⅜ in thick and 2⅞ in wide (K)
- Pine, 7⅛ in long, 1½ x 1½ in square section (L)
- 2 x pieces exterior plywood, 16¾ in long, ⅜ in thick and 16 in wide (M)
- 10 x pieces pine feather-edge board, 16 in long, ⁹⁄₁₆ in thick and 3⅜ in wide (N)
- 5 x pieces sawn pine, 3½ in long, 1 in thick and 2 in wide (O)
- Sawn pine, 1 x 1 in square section:
  6 x 11¹³⁄₁₆ in long (P),
  4 x 4¾ in long (Q),
  3 x 20¹⁵⁄₁₆ in long (R) and
  4 x 2⁷⁄₁₆ in long (S)
- Matte white exterior paint
- Clear exterior-quality varnish
- Exterior-grade PVA wood glue
- Screws, ⅝ in and 1 in
- Long screws or bolts

Tools

- Workbench with vice and bar clamps
- Pencil, ruler, square and compass
- Hand-held jigsaw
- Electric drill with a good selection of general purpose drill bits
- Screwdrivers
- Paintbrush, 1 in
- Hand saw
- Scroll saw

CONSTRUCTION DETAILS FOR THE EDWARDIAN-STYLE DOVECOTE

23⅜ in
11¹³⁄₁₆ in
7 in
5 in
2⅜ in
7⅞ in
6⅜ in
5 in
6⅜ in
35⅛ in
5 in
6⅜ in
5 in
7⁷⁄₁₆ in

Q
S
B
G

1¼ in grid

FRONT VIEW

16 in
11¹³⁄₁₆ in
9⁵⁄₁₆ in
1¼ in grid
K
O
R
2 in
7½ in
R
4¾ in
R

1¼ in grid

SIDE VIEW

Curves are
cut with
the jigsaw

Cut to fit
roof notch
(angles to
match roof)

Notch cut to
receive finial

Roof panel

FINIAL DETAIL

L (cut the finial so that it slides in place over the front of the roof)

Feather-edge boards – lap the boards one over the other like roof tiles and fix with screws

M

N

P (square-section pine screwed to the wall and floor)

D

E

C

Screw the support shelf to the brackets and the underside of the cote

A

F

H

I

J

Landing platform (the waste from cutting out a window) is screwed to the floor

Bracket fixed with two screws

Front panel with the platform support brackets screwed in place

EXPLODED VIEW

Step 1: Setting out the design

Step 2: Using the jigsaw

Step 3: Attaching the first side, floors, back and platforms

Step 4: Fitting the second side

Step 5: Attaching the front and roof boards

6: Attaching the feather-edge boards

7: Attaching the finial

Step 8: Making and fitting the support brackets

HOW TO MAKE THE PROJECT

Step 1: Setting out the design Use the pencil, ruler, square and compass to set out the panels.

Step 2: Using the jigsaw Cut out the door holes. Drill a starting hole on the bottom edge of the enclosed doors.

Step 3: Fitting the first side, floors, back and platforms Fit the first side (C), back (B) and the floors (D, E and F) together with battens (P, Q, R and S). Paint the underside of the platforms and screw them to the floors.

Step 4: Fitting the second side Screw the second side into place with the 1 inch screws.

Step 5: Attaching the front and roof boards Screw the roof boards (M) in place, and the brackets (O) to the front board. Paint and varnish the whole work. Screw the front (A) to the side boards with the 1 inch screws and screw the platforms to the brackets.

Step 6: Fitting the feather-edge boards Saw the feather-edge boards (N) to length with the hand saw, lap them one over the other and attach with the ⅝ inch screws.

Step 7: Fitting the finial Cut the finial (L) to shape with the scroll saw and then notch each side so that it slides in place on the front edge of the roof. Attach with glue.

Step 8: Making and fitting the support brackets Paint the component parts that make up the support shelf – the back board (G), the top board (H) and the angles (I and J). Attach them together with glue and the ⅝ inch screws. Finally, glue and screw (with the ⅝ inch screws) the support shelf to the underside of the dovecote.

MOUNTING

Find a position high up on a gable, under the eaves, or on a shed. Attach the dovecote about 9–13 feet above the ground, using long screws or bolts.

USEFUL ADDRESSES

US CONTACTS

The National Audobon Society
700 Broadway, New York, NY 10003

The Ornithological Council
1725 K Street, NW suite 212, Washington,
DC 20006

The American Birding Association
720 West Monument Street, Colorado Springs,
Colorado 80904

US WOODWORKING SUPPLIERS

Art & Woodcraft Supply
190 Hwy 546, West Monroe, Louisiana 71291

H.A. Stiles Company
170 Forest Street, Westbrook, ME 04092

The Wood & Shop, Inc.
5605 North Lindbergh, St. Louis, Missouri 63042

US BIRD FOOD SUPPLIERS

Agway, Inc.
P.O. Box 169, Grandin, North Dakota 58038

PetsMart
19601 N. 27th Avenue, Phoenix, Arizona 85027

Harrison's Bird Foods
220 Congress Park Drive, #232 Delray Beach,
Florida 33445

FURTHER READING

Attracting Birds to Your Garden, STEPHEN MOSS AND DAVID COTTRIDGE, New Holland, UK, 1998

Chris Packham's Back Garden Nature Reserve, New Holland, UK, Available: April 2001

Bill Oddie's Birds of Britain and Ireland, New Holland, UK, 1999

The Bird Table Book, TONY SOPER, David and Charles, UK, 1992

Creating a Wildlife Garden, BOB AND LIZ GIBBONS, Hamlyn, UK, 1988

Feed the Birds, TONY SOPER, David and Charles, UK, 1991

The Nature Observer's Handbook, JOHN W. BRAINERD, Globe Pequot Press, USA, 1986

Attracting Backyard Wildlife, WILLIAM J. MERILLEES, Voyager Press, USA, 1989

Garden Bird Facts, MARCUS SCHNECK, Barnes and Noble Books, USA, 1992

Hosting the Birds, JAN MAHNKEN, Storey Books, USA, 1989

The Natural Garden, KEN DRUSE, Clarkson, USA, 1989

INDEX

PHOTOGRAPH ACKNOWLEDGEMENTS

David Cottridge pp: 6, 8, 9, 10, 12, 13, 15, 16(r), 17; Richard Revels p 16(bl); Paul Sterry p 16(tl)